SEA TURTLE

Amazing Facts About Nature's Ocean Travelers

Dylanna Press

Copyright © 2026 by Dylanna Press

All rights reserved. No part of this publication may be reproduced, stored in a retrieval system, or transmitted by any means, including electronic, mechanical, photocopying, or otherwise, without prior written permission of the publisher.

Although the publisher has taken all reasonable care in the preparation of this book, we make no warranty about the accuracy or completeness of its content and, to the maximum extent permitted, disclaim all liability arising from its use.

Trademarks: Dylanna Press is a registered trademark of Dylanna Publishing, Inc. and may not be used without written permission.

ISBN: 978-1647904340 (pb); 978-1647904722 (hc)

Publisher: Dylanna Publishing, Inc.
First Edition: 2026
10 9 8 7 6 5 4 3 2 1

For information about special discounts for bulk purchases, please contact:

orders@dylannnapublishing.com
Dylanna Publishing, Inc.
www.dylannapublishing.com

Contents

Meet the Sea Turtle 7

What Do Sea Turtles Look Like? 8

Ocean Wanderers 11

Super Survivors – Sea Turtle Adaptations 12

What Do Sea Turtles Eat? 15

Life in the Ocean 16

The Great Journey 19

A Day in the Life 20

Nesting 23

The Race to the Sea 24

Ocean Guardians: How Sea Turtles Protect the Planet 27

Predators and Dangers 28

Challenges and Threats 31

Life Span and Population 32

Conclusion 35

Test Your Sea Turtle Knowledge! 36

STEM Challenge: Think Like a Scientist! 37

Word Search 38

Glossary 39

Resources and References 40

Index 41

Fun Fact: Sea turtles swam with the dinosaurs! They've been around for over 100 million years—and they've barely changed since then.

Meet the Sea Turtle

SPLASH! A smooth shell glides through the salty sea. Just above the waves, a small head pokes out for a breath of air. Then—WHOOSH!—it disappears again into the blue. You've just spotted one of the ocean's most ancient travelers: the sea turtle!

Sea turtles are large **reptiles** that live in warm ocean waters all around the world. You'll find them swimming near coral reefs, nesting on tropical beaches, or drifting through open seas. Florida, Mexico, and Australia are some of the most important places for sea turtle nesting.

There are **seven species** of sea turtle: the Green turtle, Loggerhead, Hawksbill, Leatherback, Kemp's ridley, Olive ridley, and Flatback turtle. All belong to a group of reptiles called **Testudines**, which includes all turtles and tortoises. Sea turtles have lived on Earth for over 100 million years—since the time of the dinosaurs!

Built for life in the ocean, sea turtles have strong flippers, smooth shells, and the ability to hold their breath for hours. But they face serious threats from pollution, climate change, and getting caught in fishing gear.

You might think of sea turtles as slow or shy, but they're actually powerful swimmers and long-distance travelers. Sea turtles are graceful, tough, and essential to ocean health. By the time you finish learning about them, you might just think they're incredible, too.

What Do Sea Turtles Look Like?

Sea turtles are living masterpieces of ocean engineering. Every part of their body has been shaped by millions of years of evolution to make them perfectly suited for life in the sea.

Size and Shape

A Green sea turtle's streamlined shell, or carapace, can measure 3 to 4 feet (0.9 to 1.2 meters) long and helps them glide effortlessly through the water. Adult Green turtles typically weigh between 240 to 420 pounds (110 to 190 kg), though some giants can reach over 500 pounds (227 kg). But sea turtles come in dramatically different sizes. The Kemp's ridley turtle weighs only 75 to 100 pounds (34 to 45 kg) and measures just 2 feet (0.6 meters) long. At the other extreme, massive Leatherback turtles can grow over 6 feet (1.8 meters) long and weigh up to 1,500 pounds (680 kg)—as much as a small car!

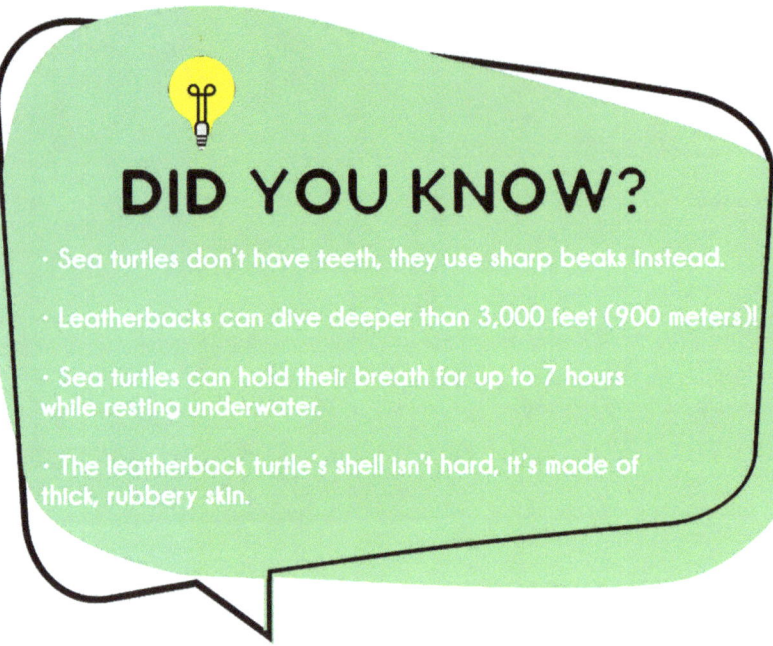

DID YOU KNOW?
- Sea turtles don't have teeth, they use sharp beaks instead.
- Leatherbacks can dive deeper than 3,000 feet (900 meters).
- Sea turtles can hold their breath for up to 7 hours while resting underwater.
- The leatherback turtle's shell isn't hard, it's made of thick, rubbery skin.

Instead of legs, sea turtles have powerful flippers that work like underwater wings. Their front flippers are much longer than their back ones, providing the main propulsion for swimming. Unlike land turtles that can pull their heads into their shells, sea turtles have relatively small heads that can't retract, but this streamlined design helps them cut through the water.

Different Designs for Different Diets

Each species has unique features that match its feeding style. Hawksbill turtles have narrow, pointed beaks perfect for reaching into coral crevices to grab sponges. Loggerheads have massive, powerful heads and strong jaws for crushing hard-shelled prey like crabs. Leatherbacks are the most unusual; instead of a hard shell, they have a flexible, leathery carapace with seven ridges that help them dive to incredible depths.

Their shells aren't just for protection—they're also shaped for swimming efficiency. The teardrop design reduces drag, while the smooth surface helps water flow around them. Most sea turtles swim at steady speeds of a few miles per hour, but when escaping danger they can burst to speeds of 20 miles per hour (32 km/h) for short distances.

Fun Fact:
Sea turtles "cry" to get rid of extra salt! Special glands behind their eyes release salty tears, helping them drink seawater without getting sick.

Ocean Wanderers

Sea turtles are true citizens of the world. They're found in warm and temperate oceans across the globe, from the Caribbean to the coasts of Japan.

Different species prefer different "ocean neighborhoods." **Green turtles** love shallow coastal waters with seagrass and algae. You'll find them grazing near coral reefs and rocky coastlines.

Loggerheads swim in both shallow waters and the open ocean, following warm currents that carry their favorite prey.

Hawksbill turtles are the coral reef specialists, spending most of their time around tropical reefs in the Atlantic, Pacific, and Indian Oceans. Their narrow heads and sharp beaks help them reach into tight spaces to grab sponges.

Leatherbacks are the ultimate explorers. These giants can dive over 4,000 feet (1,200 meters) and roam across entire oceans, even into cold waters, hunting jellyfish.

Unlike many marine animals that stay in one area, sea turtles are incredible travelers. They don't have permanent homes but instead move between different habitats throughout their lives. Young turtles might spend years drifting with ocean currents in the open sea, while adults travel between feeding areas and nesting beaches.

The ocean provides everything sea turtles need: food, shelter, highways for travel, and even nurseries for their young. Warm currents help them move across the sea, and cold upwellings create feeding hotspots.

DID YOU KNOW?

- Sea turtles use Earth's magnetic field like a built-in GPS to navigate the ocean
- Some sea turtles travel thousands of miles each year to feed or nest
- Sea turtles are found in every ocean except the Arctic

Super Survivors – Sea Turtle Adaptations

Every part of a sea turtle's body tells a story of millions of years of adaptation to ocean life. These remarkable creatures have developed some of nature's most impressive survival tools.

- **Hydrodynamic Design:** Sea turtles are living submarines. Their teardrop-shaped shells and streamlined bodies slice through water with minimal resistance. Even their flippers fold perfectly against their bodies to reduce drag during long-distance swimming.

- **Powerful Swimming Flippers:** Unlike the webbed feet of ducks or the fins of fish, sea turtle flippers work like underwater wings. They "fly" through the water using figure-eight motions that provide both lift and thrust, allowing them to glide gracefully or burst into high-speed escapes.

- **Salt Excretion System:** Special glands behind their eyes act like biological desalination plants, filtering excess salt from their blood. This allows them to drink seawater and eat salty foods without poisoning themselves—an ability that gives them access to the entire ocean.

- **Incredible Diving Ability:** Most sea turtles can hold their breath for 15-30 minutes, but Leatherbacks are diving champions, staying underwater for up to 85 minutes and reaching depths of over 4,000 feet (1,200 meters). Their hearts slow down dramatically to conserve oxygen.

- **Magnetic Navigation:** Sea turtles have built-in GPS systems that use the Earth's magnetic field for navigation. They can sense tiny changes in magnetic strength and direction, allowing them to navigate across thousands of miles of open ocean and return to the exact beaches where they were born.

- **Temperature Regulation:** As cold-blooded reptiles, sea turtles use behavioral strategies to control their body temperature. They bask at the surface in cold water and dive deep in warm water. Leatherbacks can even generate some body heat through muscle activity.

- **Specialized Feeding Equipment:** Each species has jaws and digestive systems perfectly matched to their diet. Green turtles have serrated jaws for slicing seagrass, while Loggerheads have powerful crushing jaws for hard-shelled prey.

- **Protective Shell:** Their shells aren't just armor—they're also flotation devices. The shell's design provides just enough buoyancy to help them hover effortlessly in the water column while feeding or resting.

These adaptations make sea turtles some of the most successful and wide-ranging marine reptiles on the planet.

Fun Fact: Leatherback turtles can dive deeper than 4,000 feet—that's deeper than most whales can go!

What Do Sea Turtles Eat?

Sea turtles are picky eaters with very different tastes depending on their species. Their diets are so specialized that you can often tell what kind of turtle you're looking at just by watching what it eats!

- **Green sea turtles** spend their days grazing on seagrass beds and algae. Their serrated jaws work like scissors, cutting through tough sea plants. A single adult Green turtle can eat up to 4-5 pounds (1.8-2.3 kg) of seagrass per day! But here's something surprising: juvenile Green turtles are actually omnivores, eating jellyfish, small crustaceans, fish eggs, and algae before switching to their plant-based adult diet.
- **Loggerhead turtles** have powerful jaws built for cracking hard shells. They love crabs, lobsters, shrimp, clams, and sea urchins. Their massive heads house incredibly strong jaw muscles that can crush a crab shell like we'd crack a walnut. They also eat jellyfish, fish, and squid when the opportunity arises.
- **Hawksbill turtles** are coral reef specialists with narrow, pointed beaks perfect for their favorite food: sponges. These colorful reef creatures would be toxic to most animals, but Hawksbills have special adaptations that let them safely digest sponges that other animals can't touch. They also eat sea anemones, jellyfish, and algae found around coral reefs.
- **Leatherback turtles** are the jellyfish eaters of the ocean, consuming hundreds of jellyfish per day! Their throats are lined with backward-pointing spines that help them swallow slippery jellyfish and prevent them from escaping. Leatherbacks will travel thousands of miles following jellyfish swarms across the ocean.
- The **ridley turtles (both Kemp's and Olive ridleys)** are opportunistic feeders with varied diets. They eat crabs, shrimp, fish, jellyfish, algae, and seagrass, adapting their meals to whatever's available in their habitat.

Sea turtles don't chew their food—they swallow it whole or tear it into chunks. Their stomachs are incredibly strong and can digest hard shells, tough plant material, and even the occasional accidentally swallowed trash (which is unfortunately becoming a serious problem).

Most sea turtles are daytime feeders, though some species will feed at night when certain prey is more active. They can fast for weeks or even months during long migrations, living off stored fat until they reach their feeding grounds.

BUILT TO EAT!

GREEN TURTLE — Serrated, saw-like edge — Seagrass and algae

LOGGERHEAD — Massive, crushing beak — Crabs and clams

HAWKSBILL — Sharp, narrow, bird-like — Sponges

LEATHERBACK — Soft mouth, spiny throat — Jellyfish

Life in the Ocean

Sea turtles are mostly loners, spending most of their lives swimming solo through the vast ocean. They don't form permanent groups or defend territories like many other animals. Instead, they're nomadic wanderers, moving wherever the currents, food, and seasons take them.

However, sea turtles do come together in special situations. During feeding, many turtles may gather in the same seagrass bed or jellyfish bloom without fighting. These "feeding aggregations" can include dozens of turtles, all peacefully eating side by side.

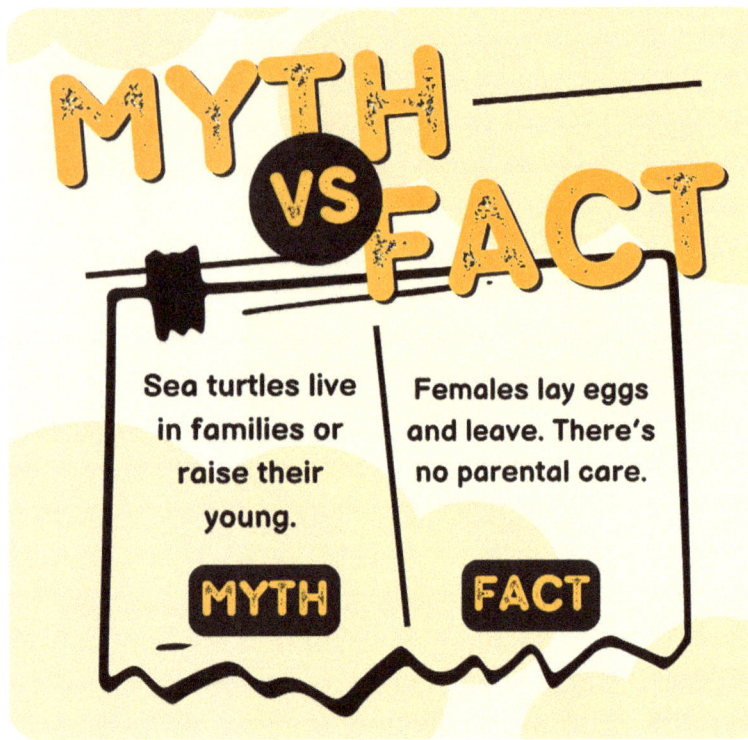

One of the most interesting social behaviors involves "cleaning stations"—areas where small fish remove algae, barnacles, and parasites from sea turtles' shells and skin. The turtles will hold perfectly still while cleaner fish like tangs and wrasses do their work, creating a beneficial relationship for both species.

Young sea turtles show more social behavior than adults. Hatchlings often swim together in groups during their first few days in the ocean, possibly providing some protection from predators. These loose associations usually break up as the young turtles disperse into different ocean currents.

Sea turtles also interact with many other marine species during their travels. They often serve as mobile homes for various small creatures like barnacles, algae, and remora fish that hitchhike on their shells. While this might seem bothersome, most of these relationships don't harm the turtle and sometimes even help by providing camouflage or cleaning services.

Despite their mostly solitary nature, sea turtles play important social roles in ocean ecosystems, connecting different marine habitats through their travels and movements.

Fun Fact: Baby sea turtles memorize the Earth's magnetic field at their birth beach—and use that "map" to find their way back decades later!

The Great Journey

Sea turtles are among nature's greatest navigators, capable of epic journeys that put human explorers to shame. These ancient mariners can travel over 10,000 miles (16,000 km) in a single year, crossing entire ocean basins with pinpoint accuracy.

What makes these journeys so remarkable isn't just the distance—it's the precision. A female Green turtle might swim from her feeding grounds off the coast of Brazil to nest on a tiny beach in West Africa, then return to the exact same feeding area. Some Loggerhead turtles hatched in Japan swim all the way across the Pacific Ocean to feeding areas off California and Mexico, then somehow find their way back to Japanese beaches to nest decades later.

How do they do it? Sea turtles have one of nature's most sophisticated navigation systems. They use Earth's magnetic field like an internal GPS, sensing tiny variations in magnetic strength and angle that change from place to place. Scientists believe baby turtles imprint on the unique magnetic signature of their birth beach, creating a magnetic map they carry for life.

But magnetic navigation is just one tool in their toolkit. Sea turtles also use ocean currents as underwater highways, riding warm currents like the Gulf Stream that can carry them thousands of miles with minimal effort. They follow temperature gradients, chemical trails, and even use the position of the sun and stars for navigation.

The timing of these migrations is often linked to food availability and breeding cycles. Leatherback turtles follow seasonal jellyfish blooms across the ocean, while Green turtles time their movements to coincide with peak seagrass growth in their feeding areas.

Some of the most incredible journeys happen during the "lost years"—the mysterious period when young turtles disappear into the open ocean for years or even decades. Recent tracking studies have revealed that juvenile turtles ride circular ocean currents called gyres, traveling vast distances while growing and maturing in the relative safety of the open sea.

These epic migrations connect distant parts of the ocean and make sea turtles truly global citizens. A single turtle might visit the waters of a dozen different countries during its lifetime, making international cooperation essential for their conservation.

A Day in the Life

Sea turtles don't follow the same daily routines as land animals, but they do have patterns of activity that change with the tides, temperature, and their individual needs.

Most are active during the day. A typical morning begins with gentle swimming near the surface, where the turtle warms up in the sun. Since they're cold-blooded, sea turtles need to absorb heat from their surroundings to become fully active.

Feeding usually takes up several hours of the day. Green turtles might spend 6-8 hours grazing on seagrass beds, moving slowly across the bottom like underwater lawn mowers. Loggerheads are more active hunters, digging through sand for shellfish or chasing crabs and fish.

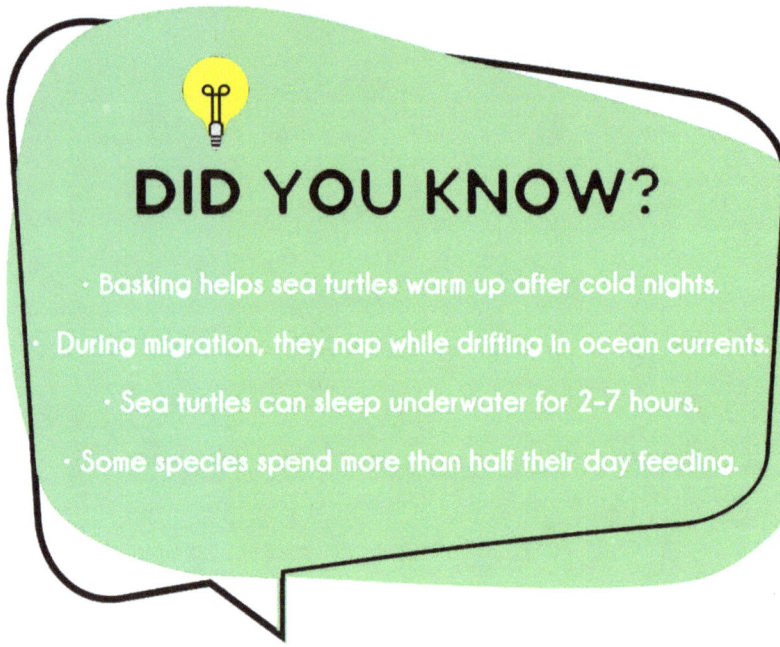

DID YOU KNOW?
- Basking helps sea turtles warm up after cold nights.
- During migration, they nap while drifting in ocean currents.
- Sea turtles can sleep underwater for 2-7 hours.
- Some species spend more than half their day feeding.

Between feedings, turtles rest underwater by tucking into coral crevices or ledges to keep from rising to the surface. While resting, their heart rate slows, and they may stay submerged for several hours.

Some sea turtles practice "basking"—floating at the surface with part of their shell exposed to the sun. This behavior is most common in cooler waters and helps them regulate their body temperature. Hawaiian Green turtles are famous for hauling out completely onto beaches to bask in the sun.

During migrations, sea turtles can swim continuously for days or weeks, taking short rest breaks while floating at the surface. They're capable of sleeping while drifting with ocean currents, essentially sleeping while traveling.

At night, most sea turtles become less active, though some species continue feeding if prey is available. The ocean is generally safer for them in darkness, as many of their predators are visual hunters that rely on daylight.

Unlike many animals with rigid daily schedules, sea turtles live by the rhythm of the ocean—responding to currents, temperatures, food availability, and the ancient migrations programmed into their DNA.

Fun Fact: A single Leatherback turtle can eat over 400 pounds of jellyfish in one day—helping keep jellyfish populations in check!

Fun Fact: A few degrees can change everything! Warmer sand produces female hatchlings, while cooler sand produces males.

Nesting

One of nature's most incredible spectacles happens on beaches around the world when female sea turtles emerge from the ocean to lay their eggs. This ancient ritual has remained unchanged for millions of years.

Female sea turtles typically don't nest until they're 15-30 years old, depending on the species. When ready, they begin a remarkable journey navigating thousands of miles to return to the exact beach where they were born. Scientists believe they use Earth's magnetic field to find their way home.

The nesting process is both tiring and dangerous. Under cover of darkness, a female turtle emerges from the waves and uses her powerful flippers to crawl up the beach above the high-tide line. This journey can take over an hour for large species like Leatherbacks, and every step is difficult because their flippers are designed for swimming, not walking.

Once she finds the perfect spot, she uses her back flippers to dig a deep, flask-shaped hole about 2 feet (60 cm) deep. This process requires patience and precision.

The egg-laying process is quick but amazing. Depending on the species, she'll lay between 50-200 ping-pong-ball-sized eggs, each covered in a leathery shell. Green turtles typically lay around 100-120 eggs, while Leatherbacks often lay fewer.

Here's the twist: the temperature of the sand determines whether the babies will be male or female! Warmer sand produces mostly females, while cooler sand produces mostly males. Rising temperatures from climate change are now affecting this delicate balance.

Afterward, the turtle carefully covers the nest with sand, often disguising it with false tracks to confuse predators. The entire process can take 3–4 hours.

Most species nest multiple times during a season, returning to shore every 2-3 weeks to lay new clutches. Some species, like ridley turtles, participate in massive synchronized nesting events called **"arribadas,"** where thousands of females nest on the same beach within a few days.

The eggs incubate in the warm sand for about 60 days, developing without any parental care—one of nature's ultimate acts of faith in the future.

The Race to the Sea

After two months in warm sand, baby sea turtles begin one of the most dangerous journeys in the animal kingdom. What happens next is a race against time, predators, and the elements that will determine which hatchlings survive to adulthood.

Hatchlings use a tiny egg tooth to break out of their shells. But they don't immediately head to the surface. Instead, all the hatchlings in a nest work together, using their combined movement to gradually dig upward through the sand. This teamwork helps them emerge together, which improves everyone's chances of survival.

Most hatchlings emerge at night when temperatures are cooler and fewer predators are active. Guided by the moon and stars, hatchlings instinctively crawl toward the brightest horizon. But artificial lights from buildings can confuse them, sending them the wrong way—a problem called **disorientation.**

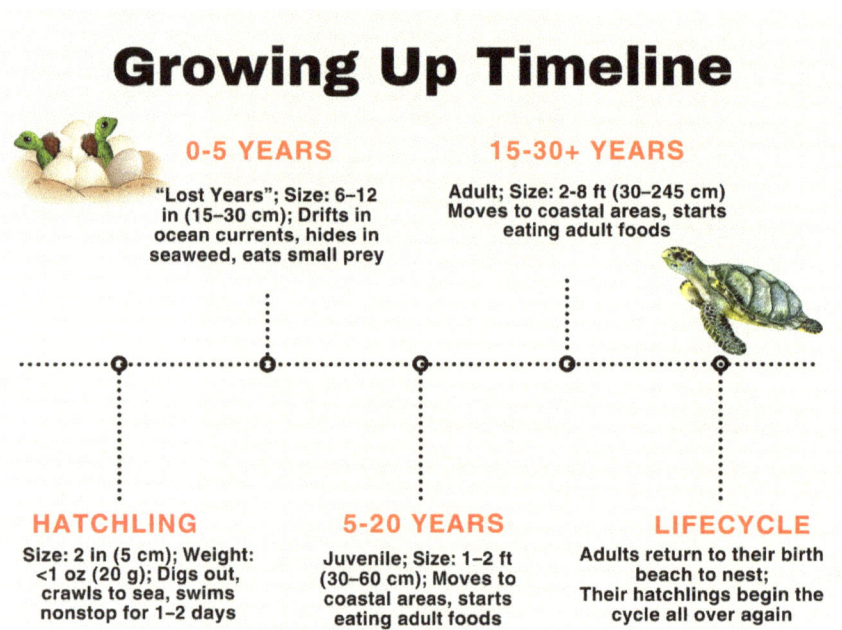

The race to the water is full of danger. These 2-inch (5 cm) babies must cross the beach while avoiding ghost crabs, birds, raccoons, and other predators. Many won't make it—less than one in 1,000 hatchlings survives to adulthood.

Once they reach the waves, the hatchlings begin a "swimming frenzy"—24 to 48 hours of nonstop paddling to escape predators near shore.

Their destination is the open ocean, where they'll spend the mysterious "lost years" of their lives. Young turtles drift in ocean currents, hiding in floating seaweed like sargassum, where they find food and shelter. In the Atlantic, many hatchlings join the Gulf Stream current system, which carries them in a giant circle around the North Atlantic Ocean.

During these lost years, young turtles grow rapidly while learning to survive in the open ocean. They eat small fish, jellyfish, and anything else they can catch. Different species have different juvenile habitats—some stay in the open ocean for 5-10 years, while others move to coastal areas sooner. Those that beat the odds and survive will one day return to the same beach where their journey began—completing an ancient circle of life.

Fun Fact: Sea turtles can sleep underwater for hours by slowing their heart rate and tucking into coral ledges to stay in place.

Ocean Guardians: How Sea Turtles Protect the Planet

Sea turtles are essential workers that help keep marine ecosystems healthy and balanced. Each species contributes in unique ways that help entire food webs thrive.

- **Seagrass Lawn Mowers:** Green sea turtles are like underwater gardeners, constantly grazing on seagrass beds. They keep seagrass short and healthy, preventing it from becoming overgrown and dying. Healthy seagrass is essential for fish nurseries, coastline protection, and storing carbon that fights climate change.

- **Jellyfish Population Control:** Leatherbacks consume hundreds of pounds of jellyfish, keeping their populations in check. Without sea turtles, jellyfish blooms could disrupt entire marine food webs, harming fish populations and making swimming dangerous for people.

- **Coral Reef Maintenance:** Hawksbills feed on sponges that can smother coral. By keeping sponge growth in check, they help coral reefs stay healthy and biodiverse.

- **Nutrient Cycling:** Sea turtles transport nutrients between different ocean habitats. They might feed in one area and travel hundreds of miles before depositing waste in another location, moving important nutrients across the ocean and even from sea to land when females come ashore to nest.

- **Beach Builders:** When female turtles nest, their eggs provide important nutrients to beach and dune plants. Even unsuccessful nests contribute organic matter that helps coastal vegetation grow, which in turn helps prevent beach erosion and creates habitat for other wildlife.

- **Mobile Ecosystems:** Sea turtles often carry barnacles, algae, and tiny animals on their shells, creating traveling ecosystems that connect distant marine communities.

- **Ocean Health Indicators:** Scientists use sea turtle populations as indicators of ocean health. Since sea turtles live long lives and travel across entire ocean basins, changes in their health often reflect broader environmental problems like pollution, climate change, or overfishing.

The loss of sea turtles would create ripple effects throughout ocean ecosystems, demonstrating how they serve as guardians of ocean health for the benefit of countless other species, including humans.

Predators and Dangers

Sea turtles face different levels of danger depending on their age and size. While adult sea turtles are large enough to intimidate most predators, their journey to adulthood is filled with natural enemies at every stage.

The danger begins even before the turtles hatch. Turtle eggs are often dug up and eaten by raccoons, foxes, feral pigs, crabs, and seabirds. On some beaches, over 90 percent of nests may be destroyed by predators before a single hatchling gets the chance to emerge.

For those that do hatch, the race to the sea is one of the most perilous moments of their lives. Hatchlings must cross open sand while avoiding ghost crabs, gulls, frigatebirds, and other animals eager for an easy meal. To improve their odds, hatchlings often emerge in large groups. This strategy, called **synchronous emergence**, overwhelms predators with numbers, increasing the chance that at least some will reach the sea. Once they enter the ocean, the threats continue. Fish, crabs, and even other sea turtles may prey on the tiny swimmers.

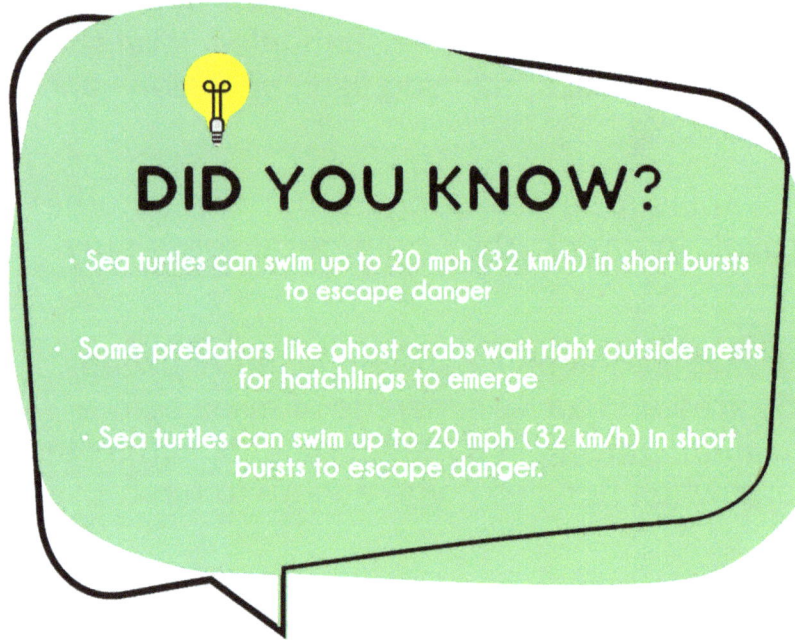

DID YOU KNOW?
- Sea turtles can swim up to 20 mph (32 km/h) in short bursts to escape danger
- Some predators like ghost crabs wait right outside nests for hatchlings to emerge
- Sea turtles can swim up to 20 mph (32 km/h) in short bursts to escape danger.

As they grow, sea turtles become better protected. Their hard shells provide strong armor against many attacks, and their excellent underwater vision and ability to sense vibrations help them detect danger early. Young turtles are still vulnerable to sharks, large fish, and seabirds, but their chances of survival improve with size and experience.

Adult sea turtles have relatively few natural predators. Large tiger sharks and bull sharks pose the greatest threat, with powerful jaws capable of cracking even an adult turtle's shell. In some regions, saltwater crocodiles may also prey on sea turtles, and large octopuses have been known to ambush turtles near reefs. However, these attacks are rare.

Fun Fact: Hatchlings enter a "swimming frenzy" the moment they hit the water—paddling nonstop for 24–48 hours to escape predators near shore!

Challenges and Threats

Sea turtles have survived for over 100 million years, but today they face threats unlike anything in their history—most of them caused by people.

Plastic pollution is one of the deadliest dangers. Sea turtles often mistake plastic bags for jellyfish. Ingested plastic can block their digestive systems and lead to starvation. Tiny bits of plastic, called microplastics, are now found in their bodies and food.

Climate change is also creating serious problems. Hotter sand produces mostly female hatchlings, causing unbalanced populations. Rising seas and stronger storms are also washing away nesting beaches. Changing ocean temperatures are shifting the location of their food.

Coastal development has taken over many nesting beaches. Artificial lights confuse hatchlings, leading them inland instead of toward the ocean. Buildings, roads, and beach traffic can also scare off nesting females.

Fishing industry impacts pose serious risks through accidental capture, known as bycatch. Sea turtles get caught in fishing nets, longlines, and crab traps. While many fisheries now use turtle-friendly gear and techniques, thousands of turtles are still injured or killed each year in fishing operations worldwide.

Boat strikes are becoming more common, especially for turtles that surface to breathe or feed. Collisions with fast-moving boats can be fatal. Even **tourism and beach activity** can cause harm. Loud noise, bright lights, and vehicles can disturb nests or cause turtles to abandon nesting attempts.

The good news is that people around the world are working to address these challenges through beach protection programs, fishing gear modifications, pollution reduction efforts, and international conservation agreements. Many of these threats can be reduced through human action and awareness.

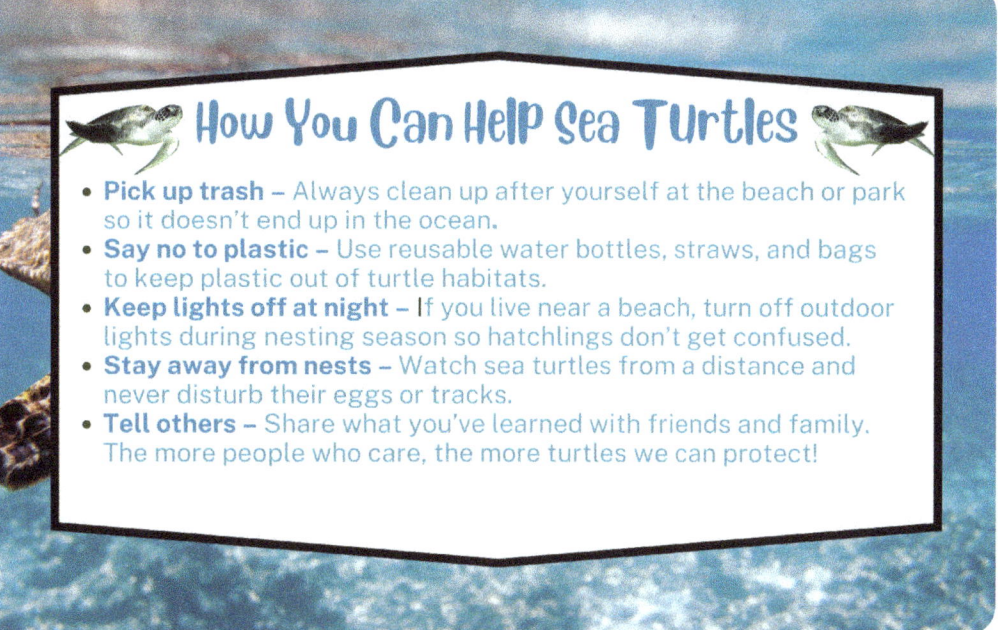

How You Can Help Sea Turtles

- **Pick up trash –** Always clean up after yourself at the beach or park so it doesn't end up in the ocean.
- **Say no to plastic –** Use reusable water bottles, straws, and bags to keep plastic out of turtle habitats.
- **Keep lights off at night –** If you live near a beach, turn off outdoor lights during nesting season so hatchlings don't get confused.
- **Stay away from nests –** Watch sea turtles from a distance and never disturb their eggs or tracks.
- **Tell others –** Share what you've learned with friends and family. The more people who care, the more turtles we can protect!

Life Span and Population

Sea turtles are among the longest-lived reptiles on Earth, with lifespans that can exceed a human lifetime. In the wild, most sea turtles live 50-80 years, though some species may live over 100 years. Green sea turtles and Hawksbills are believed to be the longest-lived, with some individuals potentially reaching 150 years or more. This incredible longevity means that sea turtles swimming in our oceans today may have hatched when our great-grandparents were children. However, determining exact ages is challenging because sea turtles don't have growth rings like trees. Scientists estimate ages by studying growth rates, reproductive maturity, and by following individual turtles over many years.

The conservation status of sea turtles varies by species, but all seven species face significant challenges. Kemp's ridley and Hawksbill turtles are listed as Critically Endangered, with very small global populations. Leatherbacks and Green sea turtles are listed as Vulnerable to Endangered depending on the population, while Loggerheads and Olive ridleys range from Vulnerable to Near Threatened.

Quick Facts

- Green sea turtles are the most common, with 200,000+ nesting females counted each year.
- Kemp's ridley turtles are the rarest—only about 7,000–9,000 females nest annually.
- Scientists estimate 6.5 million sea turtles nest globally each year—but that's just adult females!
- Nesting numbers for some species have tripled in the past 30 years thanks to conservation.
- One turtle may travel across the waters of 10 or more countries during its lifetime.

Current population estimates are difficult to determine precisely, but scientists estimate there are roughly 6.5 million sea turtles nesting worldwide each year. Green turtles have the largest populations, with over 200,000 females nesting annually worldwide. Kemp's ridley has the smallest population, with only about 7,000-9,000 nesting females per year.

Sea turtle conservation requires global cooperation because these animals travel across international boundaries throughout their lives. A turtle that nests in Costa Rica might feed in waters off California, making international collaboration essential for their protection.

Today's conservation success stories prove that with dedicated effort, international cooperation, and public support, sea turtle populations can recover and thrive for future generations to enjoy.

Conclusion

Throughout this book, we've discovered that sea turtles are far more than just ancient ocean dwellers—they're essential guardians of marine ecosystems, remarkable navigators, and living connections between the land and sea that have witnessed over 100 million years of Earth's history.

From the small Kemp's ridley to the massive Leatherback, each species of sea turtle has evolved unique adaptations that make them perfectly suited for life in the ocean. Their ability to navigate across entire ocean basins using Earth's magnetic field, dive to incredible depths, and survive on diets ranging from seagrass to jellyfish demonstrates the remarkable diversity of life in our oceans.

Sea turtles teach us about endurance, precision, and the interconnectedness of our planet's ecosystems. Their epic migrations connect distant parts of the ocean, while their feeding habits help maintain the health of seagrass beds, coral reefs, and marine food webs. They serve as living indicators of ocean health, showing us how human activities affect marine environments.

The challenges facing sea turtles today—from plastic pollution and climate change to coastal development and fishing bycatch—are also challenges facing our oceans as a whole. When we work to protect sea turtles, we're also protecting the marine ecosystems that provide food, regulate climate, and support millions of other species. Dedicated effort and international cooperation can bring species back from the brink of extinction. Beach protection programs, turtle-friendly fishing practices, and pollution reduction efforts are all making real differences in sea turtle survival.

The next time you see the ocean, remember that somewhere beneath those waves, sea turtles are continuing migrations that began millions of years ago. They carry with them the memory of ancient seas and the hope for healthy oceans in the future. By protecting sea turtles and their marine homes, we help preserve one of Earth's most remarkable success stories and ensure that future generations will share the wonder of watching these graceful giants glide through the sea.

Test Your Sea Turtle Knowledge!

Think you remember everything about these ancient ocean travelers? See how many questions you can answer!

🐢 1. How many species of sea turtle exist in the world?
A) Three B) Five C) Seven D) Nine

🐢 2. What is the name for a sea turtle's shell?
A) Plastron B) Carapace C) Scute D) Flipper

🐢 3. Which sea turtle species is the largest?
A) Green turtle B) Loggerhead C) Hawksbill D) Leatherback

🐢 4. What determines whether a sea turtle hatchling will be male or female?
A) Genetics from the parents B) The temperature of the sand C) The size of the egg D) How deep the nest is buried

🐢 5. How do sea turtles navigate across thousands of miles of ocean?
A) They follow other sea turtles B) They use Earth's magnetic field C) They only swim near coastlines D) They follow the stars

🐢 6. What is a Leatherback turtle's favorite food?
A) Seagrass B) Crabs C) Jellyfish D) Sponges

🐢 7. What is the mysterious period called when young turtles disappear into the open ocean for years?
A) The hidden years B) The lost years C) The wandering years D) The dark years

🐢 8. About how many hatchlings survive to become adults?
A) 1 in 10 B) 1 in 100 C) 1 in 1,000 D) 1 in 10,000

🐢 9. What is an "arribada"?
A) A type of sea turtle nest B) A mass nesting event where thousands of turtles nest at once C) A special migration route D) A sea turtle's first swim

🐢 10. How long can sea turtles live in the wild?
A) 10-20 years B) 20-40 years C) 50-80 years or more D) Up to 200 years

Answer Key: 1-C, 2-B, 3-D, 4-B, 5-C, 6-C, 7-B, 8-C, 9-B, 10-C

STEM Challenge: Think Like a Scientist!

Sea turtles are perfectly designed for life in the ocean. Try these fun, hands-on science experiments to discover the secrets behind their incredible adaptations!

Streamlined Shell Design

Topic: Physics & Engineering

You'll Need:
Modeling clay, bathtub or large container of water, stopwatch

What to Do:
1. Make three clay shapes: a ball, a flat disk, and a teardrop (like a turtle shell)
2. Drop each shape into the water from the same height
3. Time how long each takes to sink to the bottom
4. Try pushing each shape through the water—which moves easiest?

What You'll Learn: Sea turtle shells are teardrop-shaped to reduce drag, helping them glide through water using less energy. The streamlined design lets them swim thousands of miles without getting tired!

Temperature and Gender Experiment

Topic: Biology & Climate Science

You'll Need:
Two thermometers, two containers, sand or soil, lamp, shady spot

What to Do:
1. Fill both containers with sand and bury a thermometer in each
2. Place one container under a warm lamp, the other in a cool shady spot
3. Check temperatures every 30 minutes for 2-3 hours
4. Calculate the difference between warm and cool nests

What You'll Learn: In sea turtle nests, temperatures above 84°F (29°C) produce mostly females, while cooler temperatures produce males. Scientists worry that climate change is making beaches too hot—creating too many females and not enough males for healthy populations!

Word Search

```
H W E N A A I G P Q I E Y Z D
S L R A E C U D A O G F F A X
P K E V G N U B E A C H E T T
E C L I N G D R E O T H F J F
C A I G I J Q A R R R F P V R
I B T A L Y E J N E E F V C T
E R P T H D C L G G N O S D U
S E E I C Q Q G L F E T B V R
Q H R O T S O U L Y G R L T T
I T O N A L B L T F F C E B L
T A F H H N I S R K R I B D E
C E O Z A B E Q Z E H Z S H F
R L Y E S N Y E S H E L L H U
Y E C K F A M I G R A T I O N
L O W N O I T A V R E S N O C
D A W F F O A F L I P P E R S
H X S S A R G A E S R V K W
X H V H S G G E E I L A R O C
```

Beach	Hatchling	Nest
Conservation	Hawksbill	Ocean
Coral	Jellyfish	Reptile
Current	Leatherback	Seagrass
Eggs	Loggerhead	Shell
Endangered	Migration	Species
Flippers	Navigation	Turtle

Glossary

Adaptations – Special features or behaviors that help an animal survive in its environment.
Arribada – A mass nesting event where thousands of female sea turtles come ashore to lay eggs on the same beach within a few days.
Basking – Floating at the water's surface or resting on land to absorb heat from the sun.
Bycatch – Sea animals accidentally caught in fishing nets or gear meant for other species.
Carapace – The hard, protective upper shell of a turtle.
Climate change – Long-term shifts in global temperatures and weather patterns, largely caused by human activities.
Clutch – A group of eggs laid at one time by a female turtle.
Cold-blooded – An animal whose body temperature changes based on its surroundings, also called ectothermic.
Conservation – The protection and preservation of wildlife and natural habitats.
Ecosystem – A community of living things and their environment, all working together.
Endangered – At serious risk of extinction; very few individuals remain in the wild.
Flippers – The flat, paddle-shaped limbs sea turtles use to swim.
Gyre – A large system of circular ocean currents.
Hatchling – A baby turtle that has just emerged from its egg.
Incubation – The period when eggs develop in the warm sand before hatching.
Magnetic field – The invisible force surrounding Earth that sea turtles use for navigation.
Microplastics – Tiny pieces of broken-down plastic found throughout the ocean and inside marine animals.
Migration – A long journey animals make regularly, often to find food or breeding grounds.
Predator – An animal that hunts and eats other animals.
Reptile – A cold-blooded animal with scales that breathes air, such as turtles, snakes, and lizards.
Sargassum – Floating brown seaweed that provides food and shelter for young sea turtles in the open ocean.
Species – A group of living things that share similar characteristics and can reproduce together.
Synchronous emergence – When all hatchlings in a nest dig out and emerge together at the same time.
Testudines – The scientific order that includes all turtles and tortoises.
Vulnerable – At risk of becoming endangered if threats continue.

Resources and References

Want to learn more about sea turtles and ocean conservation? Check out these trusted books, websites, and organizations dedicated to understanding and protecting these ancient ocean travelers.

Books

Sea Turtles: A Complete Guide to Their Biology, Behavior, and Conservation by James R. Spotila — An in-depth look at sea turtle science and the people working to save them.

The Biology of Sea Turtles edited by Peter L. Lutz and John A. Musick — Detailed information about how sea turtles live, grow, and survive in the ocean.

Florida's Living Beaches by Blair and Dawn Witherington — A beautifully illustrated guide to coastal wildlife, including nesting sea turtles.

Follow the Moon Home by Philippe Cousteau and Deborah Hopkinson — A picture book about one girl's mission to protect sea turtle hatchlings from light pollution.

Websites

Sea Turtle Conservancy
www.conserveturtles.org
One of the oldest sea turtle conservation organizations in the world, with fun facts, live nest cams, and ways kids can help.

NOAA Fisheries – Sea Turtle Conservation
www.fisheries.noaa.gov/sea-turtles
Learn how scientists track and protect sea turtles across U.S. waters.

World Wildlife Fund – Sea Turtles
www.worldwildlife.org/species/sea-turtle
Explore conservation efforts and discover how sea turtles are connected to ocean health worldwide.

For Young Scientists

Smithsonian National Zoo – Sea Turtles
nationalzoo.si.edu
Explore sea turtle biology, watch videos, and discover how zoos help protect endangered species.

National Geographic Kids – Sea Turtles
kids.nationalgeographic.com/animals/reptiles/facts/sea-turtle
Fun facts, photos, and videos about all seven sea turtle species.

Keep Exploring!

If you enjoyed learning about sea turtles, discover more amazing animals in the This Incredible Planet series—from alligators to lions to puffins—and the incredible habitats they call home!

Index

A
adaptations, 12
appearance, 8
arribadas, 23

B
basking, 20
beaks, 8
boat strikes, 31
body temperature, 12

C
carapace, 8
cleaner fish, 16
climate change, 23, 31
coastal development, 31
conservation, 32
coral reefs, 27

D
daily life, 16, 20
diet, 15
digestion, 15
disorientation, 24
diving ability, 12, 13

E
ecosystems, 16, 27
egg laying, 23, 27
environment, 7, 11

F
feeding styles, 8, 12, 15, 16, 20
fishing industry, 31
flatback, 7
flippers, 8, 12
food, 15

G
gender, 23
Green turtles, 7, 8, 11, 12, 15, 19, 20, 32
growth, 24
gyres, 19

H
habitat, 7, 11
hatchlings, 22, 24, 28
Hawksbill turtles, 7, 8, 11, 15, 32

J
jellyfish, 27

K
Kemp's ridley turtles, 7, 8, 15, 32

L
Leatherback turtles, 7, 8, 11, 12, 15, 19, 21, 23
life span, 32
Loggerhead turtles, 7, 8, 11, 15, 20, 32
"lost years," 19, 24

M
magnetic field, 11, 12, 19, 23
migrations, 19, 20

N
nesting, 23, 27
nutrient cycling, 27

O
ocean currents, 11, 19, 20, 24
Olive ridley turtles, 7, 15, 32

P
physical adaptations, 12
physical characteristics, 8
plastics, 31
pollution, 31
population, 32
predators, 20, 24, 28

R
reptiles, 7

S
salt excretion, 10, 12
sargassum, 24
seagrass, 15, 20, 27
shell, 8
shells, 12
size, 8
sleep, 20, 26
social behavior, 16
species, 7
swim speed, 8
synchronous emergence, 28

T
tears, 10, 12
temperature regulation, 12
Testudines, 7
threats, 7, 28, 31
tortoise, 7
tourism, 31

www.ingramcontent.com/pod-product-compliance
Lightning Source LLC
Chambersburg PA
CBHW041646040426
R18086900002B/R180869PG42333CBX00014B/3